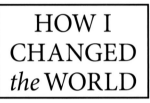

HOW I
CHANGED
the WORLD

Frida Kahlo

WORLD
BOOK

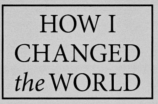

HOW I
CHANGED
the WORLD

Frida Kahlo

WORLD
BOOK

World Book, Inc.
180 North LaSalle Street
Suite 900
Chicago, Illinois 60601
USA

For information about other "How I Changed the World" titles, as well as other World Book print and digital publications, please go to **www.worldbook.com**.

For information about other World Book publications, call 1-800-WORLDBK (967-5325).

For information about sales to schools and libraries, call 1-800-975-3250 (United States) or 1-800-837-5365 (Canada).

Library of Congress Cataloging-in-Publication Data for this volume has been applied for.

How I Changed the World
ISBN: 978-0-7166-2278-9 (set, hc.)

Frida Kahlo
ISBN: 978-0-7166-2282-6 (hc.)

Also available as:
ISBN: 978-0-7166-2288-8 (e-book)

Printed in China by Shenzhen Wing King Tong Paper Products Co., Ltd., Shenzhen, Guangdong
1st printing July 2018

STAFF

Author: Kris Fankhouser

Executive Committee

President
Jim O'Rourke

Vice President and Editor in Chief
Paul A. Kobasa

Vice President, Finance
Donald D. Keller

Vice President, Marketing
Jean Lin

Vice President, International
Maksim Rutenberg

Vice President, Technology
Jason Dole

Director, Human Resources
Bev Ecker

Editorial

Director, New Print
Tom Evans

Managing Editor
Jeff De La Rosa

Editor
Mellonee Carrigan

Librarian
S. Thomas Richardson

Manager, Contracts and Compliance (Rights and Permissions)
Loranne K. Shields

Manager, Indexing Services
David Pofelski

Digital

Director, Digital Product, Development
Erika Meller

Manager, Digital Product
Jon Wills

Manufacturing/ Production

Manufacturing Manager
Anne Fritzinger

Production Specialist
Curley Hunter

Proofreader
Nathalie Strassheim

Graphics and Design

Senior Art Director
Tom Evans

Senior Designer
Don Di Sante

Media Editor
Rosalia Bledsoe

CONTENTS

CHAPTER 1

Born to Be an Artist

Childhood in the *Casa Azul*

Frida Kahlo *(FREE duh KAH loh)* was a Mexican painter whose incredibly vivid work has been described as belonging to the artistic movements called *Surrealism* and magical *realism*. (Surrealism tries to show what takes place in dreams and in the subconscious mind—a higher reality than daily life. It is characterized by unexpected arrangements and distortions of images. Realism is the attempt to portray life as it is.) A distinctive mark of Frida's work is that she seamlessly interwove fabulous elements into images deeply rooted in the real world. Many of her paintings contain references to real-life events that profoundly affected her, but the reality is presented through a lens of highly imaginative fantasy. Frida's art was inspired by the popular culture of her native country. It explores issues of gender, class, race, and identity in Mexican society. Her remarkable work expressing the *indigenous* (native) and national traditions of Mexico is celebrated throughout much of the world today.

Frida was born on July 6, 1907, in Coyoacán *(koh yoh uh KAHN)*, a small village on the outskirts of Mexico City. Her parents were Guillermo *(gee YEHR moh)* and Matilde. Guillermo was a Hungarian-German immigrant whose given name was Wilhelm *(VIHL hehlm)* Kahl. He suffered from epilepsy, which forced him to end his studies at the University of Nuremberg in 1891. Wilhelm left Germany after that and traveled to Mexico. When he arrived there, he did not speak the language and owned little more than the clothes he was wearing. Before long, however, he had a good handle on Spanish and improved his financial situation, establishing himself as a photographer. As an immigrant to Mexico, he was keenly aware of the unique beauty of his adopted home country. In 1894, he settled in Mexico permanently and began the process of becoming a Mexican citizen. Around this time, he also started using the Spanish equivalent of his name, "Guillermo Kahlo."

Matilde Calderón was born in Oaxaca *(wah HAH kuh),* a rural state in southern Mexico. Her father descended from the indigenous population of Mexico, while her mother was a *mestiza,* that is, her heritage was "mixed," both native and Spanish descent. When Guillermo and Matilde met, she was engaged to another German immigrant, but sadly he died by suicide. Guillermo had been married once before to a woman named María Cardena. She died giving birth to their third child. Shortly after María's death, Guillermo asked Matilde's father for her hand in marriage. After their wedding, Guillermo sent his two daughters he had with María, María Luisa and Margarita, to be raised in a convent.

Guillermo and Matilde had their first child, a daughter who was given her mother's name, in 1898. A second daughter,

Frida's father, Guillermo Kahlo (shown here in a self-portrait), spoiled her and lavished attention upon her. Guillermo recognized the artistic qualities the two of them shared.

Frida (right) and her sisters Cristina (left), Adriana (middle), and Matilde (back row) enjoyed a certain prosperity in Mexico. They grew up in a beautiful home and attended a local German school.

named Adriana, was born in 1902. Their third child, Frida, was born in 1907. Her full name was Magdalena Carmen Frida Kahlo y Calderón. A fourth daughter, Cristina, was born a year later. Matilde was a devoted Roman Catholic and the moral center of the Kahlo home. It was known as the *Casa Azul,* which is Spanish for "Blue House," for the bold blue color of its exterior walls. Matilde "ruled the roost" of the *Casa Azul,* and the family enjoyed a certain prosperity. Guillermo's talent at photography allowed him to establish his own studio in 1901. Three years later, he was commissioned by the Mexican government to take part in an architectural survey and became Mexico's first official photographer. Between 1904 and 1908, he traveled across the country with Porfirio Díaz *(pawr FEE rih oh DEE ahs),* the long-serving president of Mexico. Through his job with the government, Guillermo managed to save enough money to send his daughters to a local German school. It also allowed him to provide a beautiful home, the *Casa Azul*, for his wife and daughters.

Guillermo's work as a photographer provided a comfortable living for the Kahlo family. However, Frida later described the atmosphere of the *Casa Azul* as "very sad." Neither of her parents enjoyed particularly good health and both were often sick during Frida's childhood. Guillermo also spent a lot of his time occupied with work, and over time her parents' love for each other turned cold. On the other hand, Matilde's relationship with her daughters, especially Frida, was often "hot" and highly emotional. Matilde was a kind and loving mother, but she was also the disciplinarian of the home. At times, she could be cruel and, according to Frida, "fanatically religious." While Frida and her mother had their share of arguments, Guillermo spoiled his third daughter and lavished attention upon her. Frida, in return, adored her father. Guillermo saw himself in Frida more than in any of his other children. He recognized the artistic qualities that the two of them shared. "Frida is my most intelligent daughter," he would often say, beaming with pride. All in all, Frida wanted for nothing and enjoyed a normal and healthy childhood. Sadly, all that was about to change.

The Mexican Revolution

At the time of Frida's birth in 1907, Mexico had been independent for less than a hundred years, and the country was going through a tumultuous period. Its War of Independence from Spain lasted from 1810 until 1821. In the decades that followed, struggles raged for the leadership of the country. French troops invaded Mexico in the 1860's and established a puppet state known as the Second Mexican Empire, ruled by Maximilian I. By 1867, the Second Empire had been overthrown and Maximilian executed. During the French occupation, Porfirio Díaz, the man for whom Frida's father would later work, was a general in the Mexican army. Opposing the French intervention, Díaz had distinguished himself in the Battle of Puebla on May 5, 1862, and become a national hero. In 1877, he was elected the 29th president of Mexico. Except for the years 1880–1884, he would rule the country for more than 30 years, until 1911.

A masterful politician, Díaz skillfully played the factions within his government against each other. His sole purpose was to strengthen his own position. He eventually ordered the country's elections to be rigged so that he could stay in office, and, at the same time, maintain the appearance of democracy. Díaz also opened Mexico to foreign investment. The reason for this, he said, was to promote the nation's industries, expand its *infrastructure*, and improve methods of agriculture. (Infrastructure usually refers to the services and facilities that enable a country, city, or other type of community to function smoothly. These include bridges, roads, hospitals, schools, and others.) Mexico's economy flourished during Díaz's presidency, attracting scores of investors from the United States and the United Kingdom. Many new factories, roads, and dams were built throughout Mexico. However, Díaz's campaign to modernize Mexico came at the expense of the working class and the poor. Farmers complained of unfair treatment. Wealth, access to education, and positions of power within the government were concentrated in the hands of a very few, most of whom were landowners of European ancestry.

Over time, opposition to Díaz, who ruled like a dictator, slowly grew. Labor unions, which Díaz had tried to crush, joined together and organized strikes, demanding fair treatment and higher wages for their workers. Díaz responded with force, ordering the

Díaz's campaign to modernize Mexico came at the expense of the working class and the poor.

Mexican army to gun down textile workers in Vera Cruz in 1907, the same year that Frida was born. Since Díaz controlled the press, there was no mention of this in Mexico's newspapers, but discontent in the country continued to increase. In 1910, Díaz promised free and open elections. A young man named Francisco I. Madero announced his intentions to challenge Díaz for the presidency. When Díaz went back on his word and rigged the election in his favor, Madero led a revolt against Díaz, with the help of the rebel leaders Pancho Villa *(PAHN choh VEE yah)* and Emiliano Zapata *(eh mee LYAH noh sah PAH tah)*. This was the beginning of the Mexican Revolution. It would throw the country into chaos for the next decade.

It was a violent time, and the Kahlo family experienced it up close. The fighting that took place in the streets near the *Casa Azul* remained vivid in Frida's memory for the rest of her life. "The bullets just hissed," she said. "I still remember their extraordinary sound." Frida's father was most directly affected by the Revolution. When Díaz fell from power, Guillermo lost his patron in the government. One positive result that came out of this, however, was that he unexpectedly had more time to spend with Frida. The two of them grew even closer together than before. Unfortunately, this would not turn out to be a happy time for Frida, as new hardships lay just ahead.

Illness and Isolation

In 1913, when Frida was just 6 years old, she contracted polio. The disease would leave her right leg shorter and thinner than the left. Experiencing tremendous pain, Frida was confined to her bed for a period of nine months. She endured much of that time in isolation and loneliness. Unfortunately, this was the beginning of a cycle that remained with Frida for the rest of her life. When she was well enough to resume classes at her German school, Frida was treated mercilessly by her classmates. Because of her misshaped leg, they gave her the cruel nickname *pata de palo* (peg leg). Life soon became miserable for Frida. But she was too proud to let the other children know how badly she was hurt by their taunts. Frida retreated into her imagination. She imagined running through an imaginary door to a place where the playmate of her dreams waited for her.

Frida also found comfort in her relationship with her father. The two of them now had the shared bond of living with an illness. Though Guillermo often was distant with the rest of the family during the crisis of the Mexican Revolution, he always made time for Frida. Their close relationship now deepened even further. Taking his daughter to nearby parks, Guillermo helped her regain the use of her fragile right leg. The two would gather specimens on their nature walks and then return home to view them under the microscope together. Guillermo encouraged Frida to take part in sports to build up her strength, even though such activity in that day was considered "unladylike." Frida's father shared his intellectual pursuits with her as well. He taught her about literature and the works of German philosophers that he enjoyed reading. When Frida showed an interest in her father's trade, Guillermo was more than happy for her to help him develop and retouch the photographs he took. "He was an immense example to me," Frida said years later, "above all in understanding for all my problems."

Though Guillermo often was distant with the rest of the family during the crisis of the Mexican Revolution, he always made time for Frida.

By the time Frida turned 10 years old, the political situation in Mexico was beginning to calm down a bit. In 1917, a new federal constitution was announced that included sweeping reforms. Workers were given greater rights, improvements were made to the educational system, and a separation between church and state was established. Three years later, General Álvaro Obregón *(AHL vah roh oh bray GAWN)* led a revolt that overthrew the Mexican president, Venus-tiano Carranza *(vay noos TYAH noh kahr RAHN sah or kuh RAN zuh)*. Obregón set up a government that ruled Mexico until 1933. By and large, stability returned to the country, but the new government often used heavy-handed tactics to maintain its power over the Mexican people.

The National Preparatory School

In 1922, Frida, with the encouragement of her father, entered the famous National Preparatory School in Mexico City. The institution was part of the National University, which had been revived in 1910. The *Prepa*, as Frida called her new upper-class school, had only recently begun to accept female students. Frida was one of only 35 girls enrolled at the National Preparatory School, whose student body numbered 2,000. Naturally, Frida and the other girls received a great deal of attention from the male students. Frida, who by now had overcome her introversion, very much enjoyed the boys' attention.

Frida was different from the other girls at the National Preparatory School, both inside and out. While her classmates were just learning how to use their feminine charms, Frida wore her hair parted in the middle and pulled back. She also dressed in long skirts to hide her withered right leg. At the same time, the constant bullying that she had been forced to endure at her German school also left a lasting mark on Frida's personality. She had become a disobedient and rebellious young woman. She often shocked people by the vulgar language that she used and eventually developed her own personal slang, which she called *fridesco*. She was much the same way when she returned home for visits. She was determined to "march to her own beat." When it came time for family photos, for example, Frida would often dress in men's clothing, much to her mother's displeasure.

At the National Preparatory School, Frida focused on the natural sciences (such as physics, chemistry, and biology) and thought about eventually becoming a doctor. She did well academically, but Frida quickly became bored with her studies. She also annoyed many of her teachers. Every so often, she marched to the headmaster's office and demanded that one or more of them be fired for not being up to their job. However, Frida found stimulation among the school's student body. Many of her fellow students were budding intellectuals and had revolutionary ideas. Frida, who disliked most of the girls at the school, joined a small group who called themselves *Los Cachuchas,* named for the type of hat they wore. The group was made up of seven boys and one other girl besides Frida. They reflected the dangerous atmosphere of Mexico City, which was dominated by political debate. On a regular basis, hot-blooded speakers would step forward to challenge the government in power. But the challengers would either be brutally silenced or absorbed by the corruption surrounding them.

The Mexican Revolution was over, but it had lingering effects on the country—and on Frida's education and formation as a person. At the same time, despite all the progressive influences surrounding her, Frida retained something of the Roman

For family portraits, a rebellious Frida (center) would often dress in men's clothing, much to her mother's displeasure. She is shown here with her sisters and cousins.

Catholic faith her mother had passed on to her. She also maintained a deep love for the traditions of Mexico.

The leader of *Los Cachuchas* was Alejandro Gómez Arias. Arias was a charismatic young man and a talented orator. He went on to become a highly respected lawyer and political journalist. Like several other members of *Los Cachuchas,* he would play an important role in Frida's life and later became one of Mexico's leading intellectuals. Many years later, Frida paid tribute to some of *Los Cachuchas* in her portraits. Gathering at the Iberic-American Library, Arias and the other members of *Los Cachuchas* engaged in lively debate with one another, rebelling against everything that Mexican conservatives held dear. They were known to discuss the ideas of such German philosophers as Karl Marx, Georg Hegel, and Friedrich Engels. They also spent many hours reading Russian literature and putting on plays, and were well known for the mischievous pranks they played on one another.

Arias, politically motivated from an early age, gave many fiery speeches as a student at the National Preparatory School. He believed that Mexico needed a national renewal after the many upheavals the country and its people had been through. This would require bold, new leadership as well as "optimism, sacrifice, love, [and] joy." His words reflected, in part, the ideals expressed by the Communist Revolution that had spread across Russia after the overthrow of Czar Nicholas II and his family only five years earlier. Impressed by Arias's ability to inspire others, Frida fell in love with him and his ideas. She remained a lifelong—and extremely vocal—Communist. Before long, Arias became her first boyfriend. She wrote many passionate letters to him, decorating them with small drawings. In 1922, she sent him one of her earliest self-portraits.

While at the National Preparatory School, Frida met another man who would have a tremendous impact on her life, the Mexican muralist Diego Rivera (1886-1957). Many years later, the two of them would be married. When Frida first met her future husband, Rivera was a 36-year-old artist who had gained a certain measure of fame in Europe. He was trained in classical painting during his studies in there. At the same time, he dabbled in several modern techniques, such as *Cubism*. (Cubism is a style of painting, drawing, and sculpture in which objects are represented by cubes and other geometrical forms rather than by realistic details.) Diego Rivera found inspiration in the works of such masters as Francisco Goya *(GOY uh)*, Paul Cézanne *(say ZAHN)*, and Pablo Picasso *(pih KAH soh)*. To his great delight, Rivera was commissioned by Mexico City's ministry of education to produce a mural for the National Preparatory School.

Titled *Creación* (Creation), it covered over 1,600 square feet (150 square meters) of wall in the Bolivar Amphitheatre. Frida would sneak into the auditorium with her friends to watch Rivera work. She was fascinated by the man and his art.

At first, Frida played tricks on Rivera and called him *Panzón* (Fat Belly). On one occasion, she applied soap on the steps that Rivera used on his way to work, hoping to make him slip and fall. (Apparently, Rivera never fell victim to this prank, but one of Frida's schoolmasters ended up slipping on the steps, much to Frida's amusement.) Frida soon became obsessed with Rivera. She spent long hours watching him slowly fill the blank wall of the auditorium with vivid colors. Rivera was used to having people watch him work, even at this early stage of his career.

With a larger-than-life presence, Rivera was a known Communist and would often wear a gun on his hip for protection. He was overweight and had large, bulging eyes. Some people told him that he looked like a frog. His clothes were also usually wrinkled and had paint stains all over them. Although he was considered unattractive by many people, he had a reputation for being irresistible to women. By the time Rivera had finished his mural for the National Preparatory School, Frida had fallen under his spell. She even confessed to one of her friends that she intended to have Rivera's baby when the time was right.

The Accident

On Sept. 15, 1925, Frida was on her way home from school when an event took place that would drastically alter the course of her life. In the company of her boyfriend, Alejandro Gómez Arias, she boarded one of the new buses that had recently been put into service by Mexico City. The buses were made of wood and had long benches that went down both sides of the vehicle. Because the buses were new, many of their drivers were inexperienced in handling them. However, Frida liked using them because they were both colorful and convenient. Unfortunately, the bus she and Arias were on that day collided with a streetcar. The bus was crushed against a street corner, and many people were killed in the horrible accident.

Frida made this sketch (below) of the tragic bus accident that left her near death at just 18 years old. Frida, however, never produced a painting of her life-changing accident.

The scene was both gruesome and bizarre. At first, Frida did not realize what had happened to her. She was covered in blood and gold dust (which another passenger, probably a painter, had been carrying). Her only concern was to retrieve a toy that she had bought earlier in the day. Arias had been thrown from the bus upon impact and emerged from the accident almost completely unharmed. Looking for Frida amid the wreckage of the bus, he was horrified when he finally found her. She had received what appeared to be a fatal injury. An iron handrail had pierced her body and crushed her pelvis bone.

Instantly, a large crowd gathered at the site of the accident. When one of the onlookers saw Frida covered in gold dust, he thought she looked like a statue. Pointing at her, he shouted, *"La bailarina! La bailarina!"* (which means "the dancer"). Another man came to Frida's aid and convinced Arias that the handrail needed to be removed from her body. As he started to pull it out, Frida screamed in agony. The man then carried Frida to a nearby saloon and laid her on top of the pool table. A moment later, an ambulance arrived and Frida was taken to the Red Cross Hospital. There, her injuries were examined. Aside from the damage done by the handrail, Frida's spine was found to be broken in three places. Her right leg, collarbone, and several ribs were fractured, her right foot crushed, and her left shoulder dislocated. The hospital immediately notified her family, but the doctors' diagnosis was grim. At just 18 years of age, Frida was not expected to live.

CHAPTER 2

Identity and Existence

A Slow Recovery

News of the tragic accident devastated Frida's parents. By now, Guillermo and Matilde were both physically fragile people. Guillermo was deeply saddened by Frida's seemingly hopeless condition. He could not bring himself to visit his daughter for nearly three weeks. Completely overwhelmed when she heard what had happened, Matilde was "struck dumb" and never went to the hospital. Frida's sisters took the news just as hard. Adriana fainted when she was told of Frida's condition. Her eldest sister, Matilde, was the first to see Frida in the hospital and rarely left her side during her time there.

Frida's isolation and loneliness would have been unbearable if not for her sister Matilde. Ironically, Frida's accident and her time in the hospital allowed her to have something of a happy reunion with her older sibling. Matilde had not lived in the Kahlo home for the past 11 years because she had eloped against her mother's wishes. Consequently, Frida had not spent much time with her. Matilde warmed Frida's heart. With a wonderful ability to make people laugh, she charmed the doctors and nurses who took care of Frida as she sat in the chair at her sister's bedside. Unfortunately, Matilde was forced back into "exile" once Frida was well enough to return to the Kahlo home. It would be another five years before she would be allowed back into the family fold.

During the three months that she spent in the Red Cross Hospital, Frida faced her mortality every day. "Death dances around my bed," she said. Yet, once it became clear that she was going to survive her ordeal,

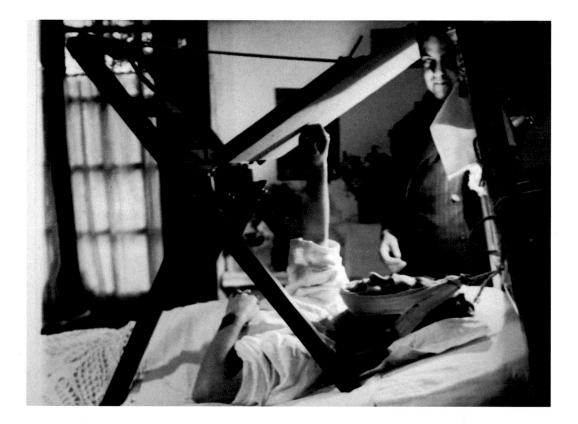

Frida realized that her dream of becoming a doctor would never come true. She went into a depression. Little by little, however, her condition and her attitude about the future improved. Before long, her incredible strength of will asserted itself and she regained the use of her legs. On December 18, Frida was discharged from the hospital and returned home. Though her doctors had done everything they could for her, she remained in terrible pain. Sometime later, X rays revealed the source of Frida's discomfort: Three of her vertebrae had been displaced in the accident and her spine had not healed properly.

Frida's time in the hospital proved to be just the beginning of her suffering. Her recovery and rehabili-

Frida used a special easel (above) rigged up so she could paint while lying in bed recuperating. Frida communicated her physical and emotional suffering and her fiery spirit through her self-portraits.

tation would prove to be long and slow. Years later, pain remained her constant companion. She underwent a series of operations to mend her right foot. She also had to wear a rigid corset to help support her spine for the rest of her life. Frida described her painful situation in a letter to her boyfriend, Alejandro Gómez Arias. "The only good side of this instrument of torture [the corset] is that I'll be able to walk again. But, since my leg will hurt terribly when I walk, there won't be anything good about it after all. Besides, I won't be able to go out in the street like that or they'll have me locked up in a loony-bin." Unable to return to the National Preparatory School, Frida was forced to

endure days of solitude at home. Her loneliness only increased when Arias left for Europe in 1927. Apparently, it was his parents' idea to separate him from Frida, who at times still appeared

After being seriously injured in a bus accident, Frida had to wear a rigid corset or plaster cast, including the ones shown below, to help support her weak spine for the rest of her life.

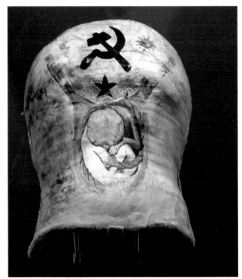

to be hovering at death's door. Within the year, Frida's relationship with Arias had come to an end and she was left feeling bitter.

During her slow recuperation, Frida's thoughts began to turn toward a career as a medical illustrator. It would combine her interest in science with her love of art. She asked her father if he would allow her to practice using his set of paints. For Guillermo, painting had been little more than a hobby, and so he happily indulged Frida. If nothing else, he thought painting would break up the monotony of her daily routine and help pass the time. He also hoped it would bring a little joy back into Frida's life. Of course, Guillermo could have no way of knowing that his daughter was about to begin an activity that would change the course of her life.

> ...*painting would break up the monotony of her daily routine and help pass the time.*

First Works of Art

With her parents' help, Frida had a specially made easel built for her that enabled her to paint in bed. It was her mother's idea to attach a mirror to her four-post bed so that she could use herself as a subject. Frida's artistic talent had failed to attract any attention at school. However, she seemed to find her calling at the lowest point of her life, when she was 19 years old. To fight against loneliness, she eagerly read all the books about art history that she could get her hands on. She also started to paint portraits of her sisters and other relatives, as well as images of life in Coyoacán. Following her mother's advice, she made several self-portraits, too. At first, Frida drew "things just as [she] saw them with [her] own eyes and nothing more." Her style was quite formal, as she was just beginning to find her own "voice." The Surrealist flair for which she is known today developed later under Diego Rivera's influence.

The praise that her paintings received from friends and family surprised Frida, and she pursued her goal with a greater passion. At first, she gave away her portraits as keepsakes, deciding who would receive them before starting the project. By 1928, she had produced a dozen paintings. Among them was her first important work, *Self-Portrait in a Velvet Dress* (1926). In it, Frida's eyes look out from beneath her now-famous eyebrows. Wearing a deep red, European-style dress, she placed herself against a dark background that looks like the sea and the sky at night. Her pose suggests an inner strength and vitality. Like many of her other early pieces, this painting clearly reveals that Frida was inspired by the masters of the Italian Renaissance, such as Sandro Botticelli *(SAHN droh bot ih CHEHL ee)*. She gave this painting to Alejandro Gómez Arias as a sign of her enduring affection. In the portrait, one of Frida's hands is reaching out, perhaps as a gesture of reconciliation to her former boyfriend.

Besides using her sisters, Adriana and Cristina, as subjects, Frida also produced paintings of friends who came by to visit her. Among them were Miguel Lira and Alicia Galant. Other early works include a group portrait of *Los Cachuchas* (1927). Though she was never formally trained as an artist, Frida's natural

abilities gave even her earliest works a unique style. Her works also demonstrated a remarkable ability to capture the likenesses of the people she was portraying. One of her more imaginative paintings was *La Adelita, Pancho Villa, and Frida.* In this work, Villa, the hero from the Mexican Revolution, appears in a painting within a painting. With unusual angles, it foreshadows Frida's later work. Surprisingly, one thing that Frida did not produce a painting of was her life-altering accident. Though she made one or two sketches that depicted the event, it remained a subject that she never committed to canvas.

A visitor at the Scuderie del Quirinale in Rome, Italy, takes a snapshot of herself with a cell phone in front of Frida's first important work, *Self-Portrait in a Velvet Dress* (1926). Frida's portrait of her boyfriend Alejandro Arias hangs on the wall at right.

Diego Rivera

By the end of 1927, Frida's confinement to her bed came to an end, and she was up and about. Once more, she began spending time with her friends from school. By now, they were attending university and absorbed in student politics. Some of them suggested that she join the Mexican Communist Party. Following their advice, Frida was introduced to a circle of new friends. Some planned to go into politics, some were *anarchists* who did not recognize any authority, and some were artists like herself. Frida drifted from group to group, exploring the fascinating world of politics and art at the same time. Eventually, she met a woman named Tina Modotti (1896-1942), an Italian actress, model, and photographer.

Modotti was politically active and a committed Communist. In 1913, at the age of 16, she left Italy to join her father in the United States. She settled in the San Francisco Bay area and pursued a career in the arts. During World War I (1914-1918) and the decade or so that followed it, many American intellectuals, artists, and writers left the United States for Mexico in search of their political ideals and a more comfortable lifestyle. Modotti followed this trend in 1922. The group of foreign-born artists that Modotti associated with would get together to analyze one another's work and enjoy life. They held a romantic vision of the Mexican peasants working in the fields. In June 1928, Modotti threw a large party to which she invited many people, including Frida. Also on the guest list that night was Frida's future husband, Diego Rivera.

Diego Rivera was much the same as Frida remembered him from six years before. Larger than life, both physically and otherwise, he was now a famous artist in his native Mexico. When Frida was introduced to Rivera, she was instantly captivated. "That was when I began to be interested in him," she later said, "although I was also afraid of him." During their chat, Frida told Rivera that they had met once before when she was a student at the National Preparatory School. Rivera was greatly surprised when he learned that

Mexican artist Diego Rivera works on a mural in Mexico City. When Frida was introduced to the famous muralist at a party in 1928, she was instantly captivated.

Frida was the little girl who had played pranks on him. As a striving young painter and a recent member of the Communist Party, Frida looked to the older Rivera for approval, and he was more than happy to oblige her.

Sometime later, while Rivera was busy at work on another mural commissioned by Mexico's City's ministry of education, Frida came by and spoke with him. "I haven't come here to flirt," she said, "even though I know you're a notorious ladies' man. I just want to show you my pictures. If you find them interesting, tell me; if not, tell me anyway because then I'll find something else to do to support my family." Rivera came down from his *scaffold* (raised platform) and looked at Frida's work. He was impressed and praised her artistic ability. He later recalled that her work showed "an unusual energy of expression, precise delineation of character, and true severity." Afterward, Frida invited Rivera to the *Casa Azul* in Coyoacán to see more of her work and, to her great surprise, he agreed to do so. Rivera was taken in by Frida's youthful grace, her lively spirit, and of course her talent. Arriving at the *Casa Azul,* he looked at the paintings Frida had there and gave his opinion on each one. Before long, the two of them became friends, and their relationship quickly developed into a romantic one.

Many considered Frida and Rivera to be an unusual couple. Twenty-one years older, Rivera was

> *Frida looked to the older Rivera for approval, and he was more than happy to oblige her.*

certainly old enough to be her father. Most likely, Frida saw something of her father in Rivera. The two men did share several things in common. Both were idealists (dreamers) and artists of a sort. Like Guillermo, Rivera maintained a certain distance from his family by working long hours, often to the point of collapse. At the same time, Frida and Rivera's relationship was somewhat reversed on another level. Frida treated Rivera in an almost maternal manner, often using the nickname *Dieguito* ("Little Diego") with him and treating him like a child. When Frida introduced Rivera to her father, Guillermo liked him and, despite their age difference, accepted their relationship. Guillermo pulled Rivera aside one day and asked him if he realized what he was getting into by courting Frida, calling her a "little devil." When Rivera claimed he knew what he was doing, Guillermo smiled and said, "All right, you've been warned." He wanted nothing but happiness for his daughter, of course, and thought that Rivera would be able to provide it. Guillermo also knew that Rivera, with his fame and wealth, would be able to support Frida, who required costly and ongoing medical treatments.

Rivera was a tremendous influence on Frida. One change that Rivera brought about was in Frida's sense of fashion. He asked her to dress in the manner of the Tehuana people, who lived in the Mexican state of Oaxaca. The Tehuanas were a

After meeting Diego Rivera, Frida began dressing in the manner of the Tehuana people of Mexico. Two Mexican women are shown below in traditional costumes from Tehuantepec.

matriarchal society, that is, women were the dominant figures of the culture instead of men. Frida responded to Rivera's request enthusiastically, in part, because she felt it would help her give voice to her *Mexicanidad*, or Mexican cultural identity. However, this change of dress served other purposes as well. It allowed Frida to express her flamboyant side while at the same time concealing the physical problems she continued to deal with after her accident. She also felt that dressing in traditional Tehuana clothing reflected her growing feminist and anticolonial beliefs. Frida's colorful and exotic new wardrobe made quite an impression on people she met at the time.

Rivera's influence became immediately apparent in Frida's artistic endeavors, which flourished under his guidance. One early example of this is her painting *The Bus* (1929). In the painting, a variety of passengers from various walks of life are shown riding

Diego Rivera's influence was reflected in Frida's early works, including the painting below titled *The Bus* (1929). A visitor views the piece at the Martin-Gropius-Bau museum in Berlin, Germany, in 2010.

along peacefully together. Among the passengers are a capitalist holding a bag of money; a stylish, working-class couple; and a barefoot indigenous woman. Surprisingly, this work reveals nothing of the fear and anxiety one might expect regarding this particular subject. In fact, it contains no specific reference to the tragic accident that forever changed Frida's life. Two other now-famous paintings that Frida produced in 1929 demonstrate her development as an artist. *Two Women* contains some elements found in Rivera's work, such as the "heroic peasant." It also has a background full of vegetation, which Frida would use repeatedly in her work. In *Portrait of Virginia (Little Girl),* Frida showed her incredible eye for detail. The little girl in the painting is wearing a dress that is held together at the top by a small safety pin, and the sleeves of the dress end in a delicate lace. Another interesting feature of this piece is that the girl has been given Frida's "birdwing" eyebrows. Rivera continued to influence his wife's work for the rest of her life, especially in her later years when her art became heavily political.

The Elephant and the Dove

On Aug. 21, 1929, Frida married Diego Rivera. She was 22 and he was 42. Only a few close friends and family members attended the ceremony at the Coyoacán City Hall, but it was covered by Mexican and international reporters. (In the coming years, the couple would be subjected to nearly constant attention by the press.) Frida's father, Guillermo, was there, but not her mother. Matilde stayed at home. She objected

to the couple's decision to have a civil service instead of a religious one in a Roman Catholic church. She also did not care for the fact that this was Rivera's third marriage. Borrowing a colorful dress and a Mexican stole from the family's maid, Frida looked beautiful. Small and fragile, she stood in stark contrast to Rivera, who was tall, overweight, and dressed in a plain gray suit. Frida's mother laughed when she saw the photograph of the couple taken that day. She said it looked like a "marriage between an elephant and a dove."

Unfortunately, the wedding was marred by several unpleasant events. Guadalupe ("Lupe') Marín, Rivera's second wife whom he had formally divorced earlier in the year, made a spectacle of herself after the ceremony ended. Raising Frida's skirt, Marín pointed to Frida's withered legs and shouted, "Do you see those two canes? That's what Diego is going to have to put up with now and he used to have my legs!" Then she angrily left the room, much to everyone's relief. The wedding party continued into the early hours of the morning. By that time, Rivera had become thoroughly drunk. He fired off his pistol in the street and even broke the finger of one of his guests. This led to a fight between him and Frida, who left the party in tears. Sadly, the newlyweds spent the first night of their marriage apart. In fact, Frida was so angry at Rivera that she refused to see him for several days.

Once they patched things up, however, Frida's life changed in ways she could never have imagined. Naturally, moving out of the *Casa Azul* and into Rivera's home at 104 Paseo de la Reforma had an

On Aug. 21, 1929, Frida married Diego Rivera. She was 22 and he was 42. Frida's mother said a photograph (left) taken of the couple that day looked like a "marriage between an elephant and a dove."

immediate impact on Frida. But there was much more to it than that. She was now married to a famous and highly controversial man. Rivera was well known as an artist, but he also remained active in Mexican politics. Everyone seemed to want a piece of him, too—the Mexican Communist Party, of which he was secretary general until 1929, as well as Mexico's conservative government. And, of course, Rivera's fame went well beyond the borders of Mexico.

After getting married to Rivera, Frida initially cut back on her own painting to be the perfect Mexican wife. Her life seemed to revolve around her new husband and making him happy. She would often make lunch baskets for him that were decorated with flowers, and climb up his scaffold to join him for the meal. For his part, Rivera kept busy during the early years of their marriage, working long days and sometimes nights. In August 1929, he was made director of the Academy of San Carlos in Mexico City. This appointment gave him great joy because he had studied art there as a young man. He introduced many changes in the school before being dismissed in mid-1930. He was also commissioned (hired) to decorate the stairwell of Mexico City's National Palace. The series of murals that Rivera painted tell a sweeping narrative of Mexican history. It begins with the time before the arrival of the Spanish Conquistadors *(kon KEES tuh dawrz),* or conquerors, and ends with events that took place in the early 1900's. The

> *Many of Frida's friends said that she turned herself into a work of art.*

series chronicles the stormy relationship between Mexico and the United States, to which Mexico lost nearly half of its territory through war. Between 1929 and 1935, Rivera worked on this masterpiece, producing three large *frescoes* (paintings on walls) that make up his Epic of the Mexican People.

During this time, Frida continued to express herself artistically, but it was usually through her colorful Tehuana-style clothing. She also wore jade, turquoise, and silver Mexican jewelry and decorated her hair with bright ribbons. Many of Frida's friends said that she turned herself into a work of art. However, Frida soon found herself with a lot of free time on her hands. Shortly before she and Rivera were married, he was expelled from the Mexican Communist Party. He was accused of collaborating with the Mexican government by taking the commission to decorate the National Palace. Frida withdrew her membership in the Party as well in support of her husband, who was deeply hurt by being forced out. Deprived of her political associations, she eventually returned to her art, producing several paintings during her first few years with Rivera. Among them were a new self-portrait and a draft of a double portrait of her and Rivera that was based on their wedding photo. She even produced a painting of Rivera's second wife, Lupe Marín. Despite Marín's behavior at their wedding, both Frida and Rivera reconciled with her and maintained a close friendship over the years. Marín would often spend time with Frida, giving her advice "from woman to woman" about how best to handle Rivera.

Late in 1929, Frida and Rivera moved to Cuernavaca *(kwehr nuh VAHK uh),* the capital and largest city in the south-central Mexican state of Morelos. Rivera had been commissioned by Dwight Morrow, the American ambassador to Mexico and father-in-law of the famous aviator Charles Lindbergh, to paint murals inside the Palace of Cortés. Named after the Spanish conqueror Hernán Cortés, the palace remains one of the oldest and best-preserved buildings in the Americas from the colonial era. As such, it was a great honor for Rivera. During the Mexican Revolution, Morelos had seen some of the heaviest fighting. This knowledge, along with the Spanish-style architecture of Cuernavaca, inspired Frida to learn more about the history of her native country. Living in Cuernavaca deepened her sense of Mexican identity. Frida's artistic style began to change. More and more, it reflected the country's folk art. Frida's identification with the people of Mexico, their culture, and history, remained a part of her art for the rest of her life.

Living in Cuernavaca was also a sad time for Frida. While there, she learned that she was pregnant but lost the child through a miscarriage about three months into her pregnancy. It was devastating for Frida. To make matters worse, she also learned that Rivera had been unfaithful to her with one of his female assistants. This was the first of Rivera's infidelities (love affairs) during their marriage. When Frida needed comfort and support to deal with the loss of their child, he wasn't there for her. Though she and Rivera tried to put the matter behind them as best they could, this was the first indication that problems lay ahead for the couple.

CHAPTER 3

Travels in the United States

First Exhibition in San Francisco

As the 1920's ended, Frida and Rivera were eager to try something new. Rivera seemed to be running out of steam, and the couple realized that the political landscape in Mexico was shifting once again. It was becoming dangerous for them to express their Communist beliefs in public, and they found themselves caught in the middle of a struggle based on their opposing world views. Not only were they no longer welcome at Communist Party Headquarters, but also the Mexican government had suddenly grown tired of Rivera's socialist-themed murals that he had painted all over the country. In 1930, Rivera received a commission to do some work in San Francisco, California, and he jumped at the opportunity. Soon he and Frida set off for the United States.

Frida and Rivera's timing was not ideal. They arrived in the United States just as the Great Depression, a worldwide economic slump, was setting in. Countless people lost their life savings, banks were closed, and many of those that remained open had to force farmers off their land because the farmers could not repay the banks for the loans the banks had made to them. Nevertheless, San Francisco welcomed them with open arms. While her husband was busy painting murals at the city's Stock Exchange and the California School of Fine Arts, Frida fell in love with San Francisco's Chinatown neighborhood and often observed the Chinese children playing in the streets. Other than that, she did not really care for San Francisco; even its scenic bay failed to inspire her. During her time in the city, Frida met several artists with whom she would become good friends. Among them was Edward Weston, one of the most groundbreaking and influential photographers in the United States. Frida shared stories with Weston about her father and his career in the field of photography. Another artist she met was Lucile Blanch, a painter and muralist. Blanch was also a recipient of the prestigious Guggenheim Fellowship in 1933. Frida also met a man named Nickolas Muray (1892-1965), a Hungarian-born photographer and Olympic fencer. Frida and Muray later became involved in a love affair.

Shortly after her arrival in San Francisco, Frida's health worsened. The tendons in her right foot and ankle had become swollen, which made it difficult for her to walk. Rivera referred her to a medical doctor—an acquaintance of his—named Leo Eloesser. During his initial exam of Frida, Dr. Eloesser discovered that her spine had been crooked from birth and that she was missing one vertebra. The two quickly developed a close friendship. Frida shared with him that Rivera had been unfaithful to her, which of course caused her a great deal of stress. Eloesser thought that the return of Frida's leg and foot problems were connected to the emotional chaos of her personal life. He recommended a healthy routine to lessen Frida's mental and physical strains. Frida appreciated Eloesser's care, and she produced a painting in his honor, titling it *Portrait of Doctor Leo Eloesser* (1931). In the painting, he stands next to a large model of a sailing ship. Eloesser remained Frida's personal physician for the rest of her life. His advice saw her through some of her worst crises.

Just as in Mexico, Rivera became absorbed in the work he was doing in California—so much so that Frida barely saw him. She kept busy by spending time with her newfound American friends. She also created several new pieces of work that reflected the change that was taking place in her personality. At the age of 23, Frida found herself outside of her own country for the first time in her life, separated from her family and friends. In many ways, despite all her thoughtful reading and political influences, Frida remained a simple young woman from the provinces of Mexico. She was forced to see the world in different ways, and her work was heavily influenced by her new surroundings. It was during this time that Frida's art began to turn toward what is known as *Fantastic Realism*. This style of painting blends the real world with fantasy. An early example of this is Frida's painting titled *Luther Burbank* (1931). Burbank was a famous and pioneering botanist who crossbred plants, created several new species, and made huge contributions to California's agriculture. In Frida's work, Burbank is represented as a cross between a man and a tree. Large leaves grow from his hands, and his legs end in a tree trunk whose roots grow out of a corpse deep beneath the ground. (Upon his death, Burbank was buried, as he requested, under a tree he had planted in his front lawn.) When Rivera saw the painting, he thought Frida was finally going beyond simple exaggeration in her art and beginning to express her own unique vision. He was pleased with his wife's progress and urged her to continue to experiment with her style.

Frida's double portrait (left) titled *Frida and Diego Rivera* (1931) is based on the couple's wedding photograph.

The six months that Frida spent in San Francisco turned out to be quite productive for her. She further developed the style she had begun to experiment with while in Cuernavaca. She also finished the work titled *Frida and Diego Rivera* (1931), the double portrait based on their wedding photo. Though she still publicly presented herself simply as Rivera's wife, Frida took a giant step forward as an artist in her own right while in San Francisco. For the first time, she was invited to put her art on public display. In 1931, the sixth annual Exhibition of the San Francisco Society of Women Artists took place in the Palace of the Legion of Honor. Frida was invited to submit *Frida and Diego Rivera* as part of the exhibit. It was one of the happiest and proudest days of her life.

One thing that Frida did not much care for during her time in the United States was American women. "I can't stand gringos," she said, using a common Spanish term for white North Americans. "They're boring and have doughy faces like unbaked rolls, especially the old women." Before long, she became homesick for her native country. As it turned out, she and her husband returned to Mexico for a short time in July so that Rivera could work on a fresco in the National Palace. Frida was overjoyed to be back home. She walked in the gardens of the *Casa Azul* and spent time with old friends.

While they were in Mexico, Rivera spoke to his friend Juan O'Gorman (1905-1982), who was a painter and architect, about a project he had in mind. He wanted O'Gorman to build two houses—a large one for himself, painted pink and white, and a smaller one for Frida, painted blue to remind her of the *Casa Azul*. He also asked for a bridge to join the two houses together. Rivera's architectural ideas expressed his understanding of—and the need for—independence in his marriage with Frida.

Unfortunately, Frida and Rivera did not have much time to enjoy being back home. In December, Rivera received an invitation from the Museum of Modern Art in New York City to oversee an exhibition of his work. It was only the second one-man show that the museum, which opened in 1929, had sponsored, and Rivera was delighted to follow in the footsteps of the French painter Henri Matisse *(ahn REE mah TEES)* (1869-1954). He and Frida soon were on their way back to the United States.

New York City

The exhibition of Rivera's work at the Museum of Modern Art consisted of 150 paintings, including pieces from his Cubist phase. Eight mural panels, which Rivera had prepared especially for the exhibit, were also shown. Nearly 60,000 people, including many well-known artists, critics from around the country, and wealthy patrons of the arts, came to view his work. All of them paid their respects to Rivera, but he could not seem to get enough of their attention. Frida enjoyed her time in New York as well, but she felt small and insignificant at Rivera's side. She was overshadowed by her husband's fame. Rivera had an international reputation while she was still struggling to find her own "voice" as an artist. The year 1931 would witness a serious development in her work, however. Besides painting the portraits of Dr. Eloesser and Luther Burbank, she also produced such works as *Portrait of Mrs. Jean Wight* and *Portrait of Lady Cristina Hastings*. While these two were commissioned works of art, Frida's portrait of Eva Frederick, a professional African American model, was something she pursued on her own.

Due to her husband's popularity, Frida was forced to go to several gala dinners and attend parties thrown for him by New York's social elite. She hated every moment of it. In the newspaper articles written at the time, Frida was referred to as "shy" and "retiring." As a side note, it was mentioned that she "did a bit of painting herself." Fortunately, Frida made friends with Rivera's assistant, Lucienne Bloch *(blok)* (1909-1999), who provided some relief from her bore-

In 1931, Frida experienced a serious development in her work. She produced several portraits, including the one she's working on at right titled *Portrait of Mrs. Jean Wight*.

dom. Born in Switzerland, Lucienne was the daughter of the famous Swiss composer Ernest Bloch and an artist in her own right. Frida and Lucienne spent much of their time together while in New York. Frida also occupied herself by writing letters to Dr. Eloesser. "The upper class is disgusting," she said in one of them. "I'm furious at these rich people here, having seen thousands of people in abject squalor."

The time that Frida spent with the upper class made a deep and lasting impact on her. Frida never really had any contact with the poverty-stricken Mexican "masses" that she championed, but the vast gap between rich and poor that she saw in New York reinforced her social and political views. It also did nothing to improve her unfavorable view of Americans. The fact that she was virtually ignored as an artist did not help either. During her time in New York, Frida found herself distracted as well. The idea of having children was constantly on her mind. Before long, she learned that she was pregnant again. The thought made her both happy and a little scared. She had a deep maternal instinct, but after the miscarriage in Cuernavaca she was afraid she would not be able to carry the child to term. These disturbing thoughts remained with her as she and Rivera prepared to leave New York.

> *The idea of having children was constantly on her mind.*

Developments in Detroit

In 1932, Frida and Rivera moved to Detroit, Michigan. Rivera had received a commission from the Ford Motor Company to paint a series of murals on modern industry in the courtyard of the Detroit Institute of Arts. While Frida did not especially care for either San Francisco or New York, her dislike of the two American cities was nothing compared to what she felt about Detroit. Rivera, on the other hand, was excited about the opportunity. He was looking forward to visiting the adopted home city of Henry Ford. As the founder of Ford Motor Company, Henry Ford had been responsible for the development of the assembly line and mass production of automobiles in the United States. Rivera, a devoted Communist, believed that industry like the kind Ford represented would free humanity from tasks that were repetitious and monotonous and lead to the creation of a better society. When he and Frida arrived in Detroit, they were met by a large gathering of newspaper correspondents. This time, Frida boldly interacted with the press. She spoke to the reporters in English, impressing them with her fluency and declaring that she, in fact, was a greater artist than her husband.

Frida found Detroit to be an ugly city and did not get along with the people she met there. She also used her second name, Carmen, during her time there. She was told that her German-sounding name would not be well received by many Americans due to recent memories of World War I and Germany's aggression on the world stage. Frida refused to change her style of dress, however. Everywhere that she went in Detroit she was met by looks of curiosity and wonder. For her part, Frida found Americans to be boring and dull. More and more, she used sarcasm, or cutting remarks, to relieve her boredom. This only became worse the longer she stayed in Detroit. Frida referred to the United States as "Gringolandia," and she complained about American culture. "The most important thing for everyone in Gringolandia is to have ambition and become 'somebody,' " she said. "Frankly, I don't have the least ambition to become anybody."

On one occasion, Frida and Rivera were invited to a dinner party at the house of Henry Ford. She disliked Ford because he was a known anti-Semite, that is, he had a strong prejudice against the Jewish people. In a childlike manner, Frida asked Ford if he had Jewish ancestry. His angry response amused her a great deal. This was not the only stand that Frida and Rivera took against anti-Semitism while in Detroit. As a famous artist, Rivera had been invited to stay at the luxurious Wardell Hotel. However, Jews were not permitted to stay there. Claiming that they were Jewish, the couple announced that they would have to find some other place to stay. Greatly embarrassed, the management of the hotel immediately revoked the ban on Jewish guests.

Once again Frida was left by herself while Rivera busily worked at the Detroit Institute of Arts. Feeling lonely, she turned to her art to keep herself occupied. She produced the painting *Showcase in Detroit* (1932),

Frida poses on a balcony overlooking Rivera Court at the Detroit Institute of Arts in Detroit, Michigan, in 1932.

which shows an odd assortment of items in a storefront window. Frida also spent some of her time with Lucienne Bloch and got to know her better, but she missed her *Dieguito*. To make matters worse, she became ill. The condition of her right foot was slowly getting worse, and she worried about her pregnancy. She was afraid that her body might not be able to

Frida had come to believe that the best way to release her sorrow was to express it through her art.

stand the stress of giving birth, and that her family's genetic tendency toward epilepsy would be inherited by her child. Her doctor in Detroit, however, advised Frida to carry her baby to term. He also suggested that she have a *caesarean section*, a medical operation in which the child is delivered by cutting through the mother's abdomen.

Unfortunately for Frida, that operation never took place. On the evening of July 4, 1932, she experienced another miscarriage. Later, Lucienne Bloch described the sad event: "There was a huge pool of blood by her bed, and she kept on losing blood on the way to the hospital. She looked so tiny, like a 12-year-old, and her [hair was] wet with her tears." Frida was rushed by ambulance to the Henry Ford Hospital. Her bleeding continued until she lost the baby. She also came close to losing her own life. Her dreams of having a child came to a tragic end. Afterward, Frida went into a deep depression. For nearly two weeks, she lay in her hospital bed, overwhelmed with grief.

Then one day, Frida asked one of her doctors to bring her some medical books with clinical illustrations of unborn babies in their mothers' bellies, along with paper and pencil to sketch the ideas that were flooding her mind. Frida had come to believe that the best way to release her sorrow was to express it through her art. The doctor, however, thought the request was strange and refused. Rivera, however, was determined to do whatever it took to make his wife happy again and brought Frida the books she had requested. Immediately, she began making sketches of babies in the *womb* (the part of a woman's body that holds the unborn child until birth). The devastating loss of Frida's second child proved to be a breakthrough in her artistic style and a turning point in her life.

The Inner Voyage of the Artist

At least two of the paintings that Frida produced around this time reflect the depth of her sorrow. One of them, *Frida and the Miscarriage* (1932), seems to be an explanation of the events leading up to the loss of her second child. In the illustration, one side of Frida's body appears to be healthy, while the other side does not. Interestingly, on the "sick" side there is a third arm whose hand is holding up an empty artist's palette. In another painting, *Henry Ford Hospital,* Frida is lying naked in a pool of blood on her hospital bed, exposed for the world to see. The size of her stomach indicates that she is still pregnant, but she is crying and her face is gray in color. The bed itself is in the middle of nowhere. The heavily industrial city of Detroit, which Frida disliked so much, is in the far-distant background. Frida's hands are bound by ribbons or strings that look like *umbilical cords* (cords that attach the unborn baby to the mother). The cords are attached to a series of strange objects, each of which represent some aspect of her miscarriage. Among them are a flower, a snail, her deformed pelvis, and a male fetus.

For the first time in her career as an artist, Frida told the story of her life through painting, revealing its most painful and private moments. She expressed herself like she never had before, finding a certain beauty even in the worst moments of her life. More and more, Frida began to explore the themes of "terror, suffering, wounds, and pain." By placing her own pain on canvas, she expressed the suffering of the world in a way that many people could relate to. She

In 1932, after experiencing her second miscarriage, Frida began to use a type of devotional painting known as the *retablo* (shown below) that expressed her Mexican cultural identity.

also used a type of painting known as the *retablo* that expressed her Mexican cultural identity. In Mexican folk art, a *retablo* is a devotional painting that uses imagery derived from traditional Roman Catholic church art (for example, Christ, the Virgin Mary, or any of the saints). *Henry Ford Hospital* is the first example of Frida's work in this style. Instead of a saint that provides healing, however, there is only a powerful embracing and acceptance of the pain and suffering that Frida experienced. When Rivera saw his wife's work, he was deeply moved. "Never before had a woman put such agonized poetry on canvas as Frida did at this time in Detroit," he said. Frida's decision to use the popular *retablo* style of Mexican folk art opened a world of possibilities for her. At last, she had found her "voice" as an artist. Taking traditional images and re-creating them, she made them new. This new style defined the work that Frida did for the rest of her life.

Taking traditional images and re-creating them, she made them new.

In the late summer of 1932, Frida received word that her mother's health had seriously declined. Matilde was dying of cancer. Immediately, Frida arranged to return to Mexico City by train. Still worried about his wife's fragile health, Rivera asked Lucienne Bloch to accompany her. The journey from Detroit was a difficult one for Frida, both physically and emotionally. Some of the things that she saw along the way, however, inspired a new piece of work. In *Self-Portrait on the Border Between Mexico and the United States*

(1932), Frida shows herself with a defiant look on her face. In one hand, she is holding the Mexican flag; in the other, a cigarette. When she finally crossed the border portrayed in that painting, Frida was relieved to leave "Gringolandia" behind her—at least for the moment. She felt that the divide between rich and poor was too great, and that most Americans seemed indifferent to the problem. She was glad to be back in her native country, which, she believed, better reflected her social and political values. More and more, Frida called herself a daughter of the Mexican Revolution. She even began to tell people that she was born in 1910, the same year that the Revolution had begun.

> *More and more, Frida called herself a daughter of the Mexican Revolution.*

When Frida and Lucienne Bloch arrived in Coyoacán, they found all the members of the Kahlo family assembled in the *Casa Azul*. Even Frida's oldest sister, Matilde, was there, having been forgiven for eloping against her mother's wishes. Frida was saddened to see how much her mother was suffering. The matriarch of the Kahlo family was in so much pain, in fact, that it was difficult for her to speak. After she died on September 15, Frida cried for days. She had hoped to spend some meaningful time with her mother during her final days, but her mother's condition did not allow for it. Later that year, Frida produced a painting in honor of her mother's memory. She called it *My Birth*. It was the only real closure that Frida could bring to the difficult relationship she had had with her mother.

CHAPTER 4

The Return to Mexico

Strained Relations

In October 1932, Frida left her family in Coyoacán and joined her husband in the United States. Rivera had received another commission in New York City, this time to paint a mural in the city's famous Rockefeller Center. He was also invited to contribute a fresco with the theme of "Industry and Machinery" for the Chicago World's Fair to be held the following year. Frida was not thrilled about returning to the United States. She did not especially like New York's urban sprawl (though she preferred it over Detroit). At the same time, however, she felt it was important to show support for her husband. While in New York, she began the painting *My Dress Hangs There* (1933) as her statement on American cultural and spiritual shallowness and a way to deal with her homesickness. It was the only painting Frida worked on during the time she and Rivera spent in New York.

The Riveras' time in New York came to an abrupt and unexpected end when Diego showed his work-in-progress, titled *Man at the Crossroads,* to Nelson Rockefeller, the young philanthropist who had commissioned him for the job. (A philanthropist is a person who gives sizable donations of money to worthy causes.) In the mural, Rivera had portrayed Vladimir Lenin, the former leader of the Soviet Union, and the heroic working class on one side, with the well-to-do upper class on the opposite side. The clear Communist message offended the 24-year-old Rockefeller, a wealthy businessman and aspiring politician (in 1974, he became the 41st vice president of the United States). He immediately fired Rivera and

Mexican muralist Diego Rivera (left) works on a mural at Rockefeller Center in New York City in 1934. The unfinished mural was later destroyed because of its Communist message.

ordered the unfinished mural to be painted over. Though his work was destroyed, Rivera later re-created the mural in Mexico City's Palacio de Bellas Artes, titling it *Man, Controller of the Universe*. For the moment, however, Rivera found himself out of work in the United States.

All that Frida cared about, however, was returning to Mexico. She argued with her husband again and again about the need to do so. Wanting to stay in the United States, Rivera responded to Frida's pleas with outbursts of anger. Many times, he walked out on her, slamming the door behind him and not returning until the following day. In the end, Frida won the argument. A group of artists, including the sculptor Louise Nevelson, helped come up with the necessary funds for Frida and Rivera to return home. On December 20, 1933, the couple boarded the SS *Oriente* and sailed for Mexico. Frida was both relieved and excited to be going back.

Unfortunately, the strain in Frida's relationship with Rivera was about to get much worse. The miscarriage, her husband's infidelity (unfaithfulness), the death of Frida's mother, and being removed from friends and family had taken a toll on the couple. Their life together had been full of excitement, but they had been apart from each other for a good deal of their marriage, pursuing their own separate goals. Unlike his wife, Rivera was not pleased to be back in Mexico and took his frustrations out on Frida. He felt he had been treated unfairly in New York and was afraid the Mexican government would once again question his every move. Feeling resentful, he blamed Frida for his unhappy situation. In Rivera's mind, his lack of success in New York was all her fault, and he never grew tired of telling her so. He also refused to produce new art, saying that all his previous work was no good. In addition, he became ill. Rivera remained entirely disagreeable until November 1934, when he resumed work on his murals in the National Palace.

A Series of Affairs

Frida was happy to be back in Mexico, but her health remained a problem. Her right foot continued to bother her. All five of her toes had become infected with *gangrene* (dead tissue due to loss of blood supply) and ultimately had to be amputated. She also required an *appendectomy*, a surgical operation to remove her appendix, in 1934. Frida produced no new paintings that year, and only two the following year. Also in 1934, the house that Rivera had hired his friend Juan O'Gorman to build was finished, and the couple moved into the San Ángel neighborhood of Mexico City. Frida imagined—and hoped—that happy times lay ahead for her and Rivera, but it was not to be. Shortly after they moved into their new home, Rivera began a love affair with Frida's younger sister, Cristina.

When Frida learned about the affair in 1935, it had a devastating effect on her. Two of the people whom she loved most in the world had seemingly turned against her. Frida adored Rivera and had always been fond of Cristina, but she felt betrayed by them. In her mind, the situation was made worse because of her poor health. She believed Rivera had found in her

In 1934, shortly after Frida (left) and Diego Rivera moved into their new home (below right) in Mexico City, Rivera began a love affair with Frida's younger sister, Cristina.

younger sister the things that she did not have—good health and the ability to bear children. However, Frida also knew that Cristina lacked her intelligence, wit, and fiery spirit—everything that had drawn Rivera to her back in 1928. Consequently, she knew the affair would not last. This provided little comfort at the time, however, and it remained one of the greatest humiliations of Frida's life.

> *Rivera's infidelity and betrayal would have a tremendous impact on her career.*

Aggravating the insult to Frida, Rivera created a mural titled *Mexico, Today and Tomorrow* in which he depicted both Frida and Cristina. In the work, Cristina is portrayed as an elegantly dressed woman. She is self-assured, quite beautiful, and surrounded by her children, while Frida is positioned behind her sister and looks unattractive and less significant. Heartbroken over her failing marriage, Frida cut her hair short, a traditional way for Mexican women to mourn. For a time, she stopped wearing the Tehuana-style dresses that Rivera liked so much and began to wear men's clothing, just as she had as a rebellious girl. She also wrote to Dr. Eloesser, revealing the depth of her sadness. "The situation with Diego is getting worse every day," she said in one of her letters. "I know I'm to blame for much that has happened because at the outset I didn't understand what he really wanted. … I'm so down and discouraged now, so unhappy that I don't know how I'm to go on. … [I]t's costing me so much to put up with all this and you can't imagine how much I'm suffering."

In a strange way, however, Rivera's infidelity was a liberating experience for Frida as well. It demonstrated that her ideas of traditional marriage, in which a wife's needs and desires become secondary to those of her husband, were holding her back as an artist. The fact that Rivera seemed unaware of Frida's sacrifice was not a basis for a healthy relationship either. When she moved out of the house in San Ángel, Frida also left behind the last limitations of social customs— both as a woman and as an artist. Rivera's infidelity and betrayal would have a tremendous impact on her career. The intense emotions she experienced in 1935 allowed her to give full expression to her artistic vision. Over the next decade, she would create some of her greatest works of art, and she would gain worldwide fame.

Frida found a small apartment on the Avenida Insurgentes and tried to move on with her life and focus on her art. Then one day she spotted her sister Cristina at a nearby gas station. As her new residence was on the other side of Mexico City, Frida was surprised to find her younger sibling there. She approached Cristina, and the two sisters began to talk. Before long, they had put the past behind them and were once again on friendly terms. Cristina also managed to convince Frida to reconcile with Rivera. By the end of 1935, Frida had moved back into her home in San Ángel. Ironically, it was not long before she and Cristina were closer than ever before.

One of the paintings that Frida finished in 1935 was *A Few Small Nips*. It was inspired by a violent, real-life murder that filled the newspapers in Mexico at the time. A man had killed his girlfriend in a drunken rage, stabbing her with a knife more than 20 times. Frida took the title from something the man said in his defense during his trial. Claiming he was innocent of his girlfriend's murder, he explained that all he had done was give her "a few small nips." In the painting, the female victim is lying in bed with her killer standing over her with a knife in his hand. The sheets, the man's clothes, and the floor are all covered in blood. Hovering above the bed are two birds—one appears to be a white dove of peace, and the other, a black-feathered raven. In their beaks, they hold a banner that bears the title of the work. The painting remains one of her best-known pieces. Frida later said that the painting captured the intense feelings of pain that Rivera's affair with Cristina had caused her. In a

A visitor looks at Frida's *Self-Portrait with Monkey* (1938), which she completed before leaving New York City. It was the first of many replicas she would make of her work over the years.

strange way, bringing the gruesome scene to life seemed to help Frida put Rivera and Cristina's affair behind her.

Something else that helped Frida move on with her life was having love affairs of her own—with both men and women. She accepted the fact that Rivera was never going to be faithful to her and decided that she had the right to do as she pleased as well. From that time forward, she seemed to give in to all her impulses. Rivera's jealousy forced her to keep her affairs quiet, even though he never bothered to hide his own. Usually, Frida pursued people she thought would help further her career as an artist. Her first known affair was with Ignacio Aguirre (1900-1990), a Mexican painter, engraver, and novelist. Aguirre described her as "scandalously beautiful."

Another man with whom Frida became romantically involved was Isamu Noguchi (1904-1988), a Japanese American artist, sculptor, and landscape architect. At the time, Noguchi was living in Mexico on a Guggenheim Fellowship grant and working with Rivera on a series of murals at the Abelardo L. Rodríguez Market in Mexico City. Frida deeply cared for Noguchi. He had comforted her at a difficult time in her life and helped to restore her belief in her artistic abilities. Their affair did not last long, however. Whenever they were together, the two were afraid of running into Rivera. Frida knew that her husband, as jealous as he was, would never tolerate another man competing for her affections. Both she and Noguchi were familiar with Rivera's temper as well, and he was still known to wear a pistol on his hip.

Leon Trotsky

In 1936, Frida had another major surgery, as her health continued to be a problem. This time, she went to the American British Cowdray Hospital in Mexico City. Because hospitals were becoming a regular part of Frida's life, they appeared more and more in her art. While she was recuperating at home, Rivera became more involved in international politics. He had spoken out publicly, as early as 1933, in favor of Leon Trotsky (1879-1940), a leader of the Russian Revolution and a former Soviet politician who was now living in exile. Trotsky had been the second most powerful man in the Soviet Union behind Lenin. After Lenin died in 1924, there was a power struggle. Trotsky lost the leadership to Joseph Stalin, who became General Secretary of the Soviet Union and accused Trotsky of treason against the state.

In 1929, Trotsky was forced to leave Russia. However, threats against Trotsky's life continued to increase. He and his wife, Natalia Sedova, lived in several countries as they sought to avoid Stalin's murderous agents. In Norway, the couple attempted to gain asylum, a formal protection granted to people who have left their native country for political reasons. However, they were turned away by the Norwegian government. When Rivera heard of this, he called upon the Mexican president, Lázaro Cárdenas, and personally asked if he would grant Trotsky and his wife asylum. Cárdenas agreed, and arrangements were made for Trotsky to travel to Mexico.

On January 9, 1937, Trotsky, his wife, and his assistant, Jean van Heijenoort, arrived in secret in the

Mexican port city of Tampico. On hand to welcome them was Max Shachtman (1904-1972), the leader of the American Communist Committee. Standing at his side was Frida. She had come in her husband's place, as Rivera was recovering from a bout of illness. By the time Trotsky's party arrived in Mexico City on a train specially arranged by the government, however, Rivera was there to greet them. Trotsky, his wife, and assistant were then escorted to the Kahlo family home in Coyoacán. At the *Casa Azul,* Trotsky was greeted by a gathering of his supporters. When Guillermo saw his house full of strangers, he took Frida aside and asked her what was going on. Trotsky and

Frida (center) welcomed the exiled Soviet politician Leon Trotsky (second from right) and his wife upon their arrival in Mexico in 1937.

his wife stayed as Guillermo's guests in the *Casa Azul* until 1939.

Frida was fascinated by Trotsky. Since her childhood, she had read books full of revolutionary ideas and had been attracted to older, worldly men. Trotsky represented both of these interests. Frida could not help but try to charm him with her ways, and Trotsky responded positively to her flirtatious manner. Trotsky found Frida to be a proud, intelligent, and self-confident young woman. Before long, the two were romantically involved. At the time, Trotsky and Frida were 57 and 29 years old, respectively. Cristina supported her sister's affair and allowed the couple to use her house. Frida and Trotsky managed to keep their romance secret from Rivera, but when Natalia Sedova found out about it, she quite understandably did not take it well. At that point, both Frida and Trotsky stepped back from their relationship. "Frida felt herself under an obligation to Diego," Trotsky's secretary, van Heijenoort, later explained, "and Trotsky felt the same about Natalia."

Like Frida's brief affair with Noguchi, her relationship with Trotsky did not last long either. It was over by the end of July, though it was never clear to Frida and Trotsky's associates who ultimately ended the affair. Some speculated that it was simply Frida's way of taking revenge on Rivera for his own affair with Cristina. Frida and Trotsky remained friends, however. On November 7, 1937, she gave him one of her paintings as a birthday present. Titled *Portrait Dedicated to Leon Trotsky*, it portrays Frida as an elegantly dressed colonial aristocrat. Many have perceived this work to be one of Frida's "inside jokes." One of the few criticisms that she had of Trotsky was his old-fashioned conservatism. Even though he was a Russian revolutionary, he often complained of Frida's rebellious and "unladylike" ways.

Experiments in Surrealism

The year 1937 proved to be just the beginning of one of Frida's most productive phases. Over the next two years, she painted some of her best-known masterpieces. *My Nurse and I* is a self-portrait that recalls the indigenous woman who breastfed Frida as a baby, about whom Frida remembered very little. The woman's face is covered by a monstrous mask that suggests art of the pre-Columbian era, that is, the time before Christopher Columbus came to the Americas. Frida is shown nursing from the breast of this representation of Mexican culture. Her adult face appears peaceful atop an infant's body. In the background, rain is falling from a darkened sky to make the ground ready for growing crops.

That same year, Frida produced several other paintings that dealt with the theme of childhood. One painting, *The Deceased Dimas Rosas,* was a "face of death" portrait that shows a dead child whom Frida had personally known. Dimas Rosas was the son of one of Rivera's friends. When the boy fell ill, his father had tried several folk remedies to cure him. Both Frida and Rivera urged the father to seek modern medical attention, but he refused to heed their advice and his son died at the age of three. Frida's sadness at the death of the young Dimas Rosas is apparent in her work.

Frida also painted several pieces that featured dolls. She had a large doll collection through which she expressed her powerful maternal instincts that were ultimately unfulfilled. In *Me and My Doll* (1937), Frida portrays herself sitting on a bed with a European-style doll the size of an infant. The two are turned slightly toward each other, but there is no intimacy or relationship between them. She is also smoking, a habit that she often captured in her art. Frida's sadness at never having a child of her own is expressed in another work titled *Girl with a Death Mask* (1938). In the painting, a small child holds a yellow flower in her hand and wears a skull-like mask. A second mask lies on the ground near the child's bare feet. All are references to the Mexican festival *Día de los Muertos* ("Day of the Dead"). Frida also had several pets. Over the years, she had monkeys, parrots, and many other domesticated animals. One of the monkeys was named Fulang-Chang, which she included in the painting *Fulang-Chang and I* (1937).

In 1937, Frida was invited to take part in a public art exhibition held at the Social Action Department Gallery of the University of Mexico. She submitted *My Parents, My Grandparents, and I,* which she had painted the year before. It gained her a lot of attention as an artist in her own right. That same year, she also sold her first paintings. The buyer was the American actor Edward G. Robinson, known for his roles as a gangster during Hollywood's Golden Age. Robinson, who was visiting Rivera's studio in Mexico City, was shown Frida's work and fell in love with it. He bought four of her paintings for $800. Also in 1937, Frida produced her *Portrait of Diego Rivera,* the only portrait she ever made of the man she loved.

Around this time, Frida met André Breton *(ahn DRAY bruh TAWN)* (1896-1966), the French writer and poet who became known as the founder of Surrealism. Breton and his wife, Jacqueline, came to Mexico to show their support for Trotsky. The Bretons, the Trotskys, and the Riveras quickly became friends. When the French artist saw Frida's work, he was impressed by it. He once described it as "a colored ribbon around a bomb." Recognizing a kindred spirit in her, Breton immediately identified Frida as a member of the Surrealist movement. Frida, however, did

Frida had several pets, including monkeys and parrots, over the years. She featured one of the monkeys in the painting *Fulang-Chang and I* (1937). She is shown at right holding a pet monkey.

not care for the Surrealist label, preferring to think of herself as one of a kind.

Two of Frida's works that made her a Surrealist in Breton's eyes were *Four Inhabitants of Mexico* and *What the Water Gave Me,* both of which were completed in 1938. Both use seemingly unconnected images to construct a narrative. In *Four Inhabitants of Mexico,* the narrative is a political one. The four principal figures depicted in the painting are a skeleton, a pre-Columbian idol, a little girl, and an effigy (image) of Judas Iscariot, the man who betrayed Jesus. In the background, a fifth figure, a piñata, can be seen. Three of the figures are festive, one represents the Mexico of old, and one symbolizes modern Mexico. (The effigy of Judas and the skeleton also appear in her 1940 work, *The Wounded Table*). In *What the Water Gave Me,* Frida captured a strange assortment of images that occurred to her one day while taking a bath. The images include her parents' wedding, a skyscraper rising out of a volcano, and her own feet with painted nails emerging from the water.

In 1938, Breton helped to arrange Frida's first solo exhibition of her art. It took place in early November in New York City's famous Julien Levy Gallery. Frida was not excited about returning to the United States, but she knew she could not afford to pass up this opportunity. Her work was well received, especially *Fulang-Chang and I.* In fact, Anson Conger Goodyear, the president of the Museum of Modern Art, asked Frida if he could buy it. When Frida told him that she had already promised it to someone else, he commissioned her to paint another. Frida completed her

Self-Portrait with Monkey (1938) for Goodyear before leaving New York. This would be the first of many replicas Frida would make of her work over the years.

Another of Frida's most famous works produced during this time is *The Suicide of Dorothy Hale* (1938). The American writer and future politician Clare Boothe Luce approached Frida about doing a painting in Dorothy Hale's memory. The mother of one of Luce's close friends, Hale had killed herself by jumping out of a skyscraper in New York City. Frida happily took the commission, but the final product was not what her client was expecting. Frida had decided to show the moment of Hale's death. The skyscraper, the fall through the air, and Hale's dead face staring out of the painting are all present. When Luce saw the finished piece, she declared she never wanted to see it again and gave it to a friend. Unfortunately, *The Suicide of Dorothy Hale* went unseen for decades. While Frida had come into her own as an artist, she had yet to grasp the commercial potential of her work.

In 1939, Frida went to Paris for Breton's exhibition "Mexique." It opened on March 10 to good reviews. The Louvre museum even bought one of Frida's self-portraits, *The Frame* (c. 1938), making her the first Mexican artist to be featured in its collection. Not even Diego Rivera had achieved such a distinction. Though perhaps a bit jealous, he remained supportive of Frida, writing a letter to the American art critic Sam A. Lewisohn: "I recommend her to you, not as a husband but as an enthusiastic admirer of her work, which is … hard as steel and as fine as butterfly wings, gentle like a lovely smile and as brutal as life is bitter."

Divorce and Remarriage

Though Rivera did everything he could to support Frida's career as an artist, their personal relationship remained troubled. Rivera's affairs continued to hurt Frida terribly and, after many arguments, he suggested they get divorced. Once again, she turned her pain into a work of art, producing one of her great masterpieces, *The Two Fridas* (1939). One of her most extraordinary self-portraits, it shows the artist as two separate women who share the same heart. One of them, wearing a white Victorian-style dress, reflects Frida's European background; the other, wearing a Tehuana-style dress, represents her Mexican upbringing. The European Frida is shown with a surgical clamp in her hand, attempting to close a severed artery. This perhaps implies that the Frida independent of Rivera's influence possesses the means of survival.

While her marriage to Rivera was coming to an end, Frida lost one of her dear friends and former lovers, Leon Trotsky. Early in 1939, he and Rivera had a falling-out following a series of personal and political differences. This led Rivera to leave the Fourth International, a worldwide Communist organization founded by Trotsky the year before. Turning to Frida, Trotsky hoped that she would intercede on his behalf. He was taken by surprise, however, when she sided with Rivera. Whatever their differences, Frida never failed to support her husband. Trotsky was deeply hurt by her actions and left the *Casa Azul* soon afterward. Once he was gone, Frida moved out of the home she shared with Rivera and back into the *Casa Azul* with her father.

Unfortunately, the break between Trotsky and the Riveras would never have a chance to heal. Agents of the Soviet Union were closing in on Trotsky. On May 24, 1940, an attempt was made on his life, but it was unsuccessful. The would-be assassin was David Alfaro Siqueiros, a painter and, like Rivera, one of the founders of the Mexican muralist movement. Though Siqueiros failed to kill Trotsky, another man finished the job. On August 20, Ramón Mercader, a Spanish Communist and member of the Soviet secret police, assassinated Trotsky in Mexico City, stabbing him with an ice pick. Trotsky died of his wounds the next evening. Mercader spent 20 years in a Mexican prison for the murder, but Stalin awarded him the Order of Lenin for his service to the Soviet Union.

On Dec. 8, 1940, Frida and Diego Rivera were remarried in San Francisco, just over a year after their first marriage ended in divorce. The couple are shown below applying for a marriage license.

Unfortunately for Frida, she knew Mercader. In fact, she had been the one to let him into Trotsky's life, having met him once while she was in Paris. For this reason, Mexican authorities suspected Frida of having taken part in Trotsky's assassination. Both she and her sister Cristina were questioned by the police for 12 hours. Not wanting to have anything to do with the investigation, Rivera fled to the United States. On November 6, 1939, Rivera's and Frida's marriage officially ended in divorce. Frida suffered terribly after his departure, both physically and emotionally. Yet again, she turned to her art to cope with life's difficulties, painting some of her best-known pieces. These included *Self-Portrait with Thorn Necklace and Hummingbird* and *Self-Portrait with Cropped Hair,* both produced in 1940. The *Cropped Hair* painting was most likely an attempt to wound Rivera. Just as in 1935 when she found out about his affair with Cristina, Frida once again cut her hair short, knowing that Rivera loved her long hair.

Nevertheless, Frida slowly sank into a depression. She began to drink heavily, and her health began to decline. Turning to her doctors in Mexico, she was giv- en all sorts of medical advice—to the point that she did not know what to do. In September 1940, she traveled to San Francisco. There, she saw her friend, Dr. Eloesser, who diagnosed her as suffering from exhaustion and alcoholism. Eloesser also explained to Frida that her ill health had been brought on, in part, by her divorce. He suggested a reconciliation with Rivera, and he served as the couple's mediator. On December 8, 1940, the elephant and the dove were remarried in San Francisco.

CHAPTER 5

Success at Home and Abroad

Recognition in Mexico

The years that followed Frida and Rivera's second marriage were generally happy times for the couple. Frida gained increasing fame as an artist, though her health continued to be a problem. In the first half of the 1940's, she took part in many exhibitions in Mexico and the United States. For better or worse, the pattern of her relationship with Rivera remained the same as before. He kept having love affairs, with little concern about hiding them from his wife. When she found out about them, Frida was always hurt and angered. They had countless arguments about Rivera's unfaithfulness. Frida continued to have affairs as well, but she did her best to conceal them from her jealous husband. Through it all, the two of them supported each other the best way they knew how and maintained a deep admiration of each other's work.

Much of the art that Frida produced during this period reflected her happiness. She celebrated her renewed relationship with the man she loved in her *Self-Portrait with Braid* (1941). In it, Frida's hair is braided above her head in the shape of a pretzel, perhaps implying that she intended to do everything she could to strengthen the bonds between herself and Rivera. Unfortunately, Frida's happy time did not last long. On April 14, 1941, Guillermo Kahlo died in Mexico City at the age of 69. The death of her father devastated Frida, so much so that it would be 10 years before she found the strength to paint *Portrait of Don Guillermo Kahlo* (1951) in his honor. Upon her father's death, the *Casa Azul* became Frida's home. After finishing a commission in the United States, Rivera also moved into the *Casa Azul* to be with Frida. From that point on, he would use his house in San Ángel only as a studio and a place of retreat. Shortly afterward, he began work on a series of frescoes in the courtyard of the National Palace. He finished the work, known as *Precolonial and Colonial Mexico,* in 1951.

That same year, Rivera began an ambitious project to gather his enormous collection of pre-Columbian art and artifacts. He invested every peso he had into this venture, and he worked on it until his death in 1957. He designed the pyramid-like Anahuacalli Museum, as it came to be known, to house his collection. The museum was built on a dry tract of land known as the Pedregal (meaning "stony ground" in Spanish).

Frida and Diego Rivera stand together with a pet monkey in front of a thatched-roof hut which houses many archaeological artifacts from Rivera's massive collection.

Diego Rivera (right) watches his wife work on a self-portrait in Mexico City. In 1942, Frida's work was included in an exhibition at the Museum of Modern Art in New York City.

Frida wholeheartedly supported her husband's idea. She even went to the Mexican government for funds, promising that the museum would be handed over to the government upon Rivera's death. It was also the couple's intention to establish a farm in the Pedregal where they could grow their own food.

Frida's fame continued to grow in both the United States and Europe. In 1942, her work was included in an exhibition called "Twentieth-Century Portraits" at the Museum of Modern Art in New York City. She submitted *Self-Portrait with Braid* and received wonderful reviews. In January 1943, she participated in a show of works by 31 female artists at Peggy Guggen-heim's Art of This Century Gallery. This was followed by an exhibit of Mexican modern art at the Museum of Fine Art in Philadelphia, Pennsylvania, later that year. At the same time, Frida began to achieve greater status in her native Mexico. Demand for her work, especially portraits, slowly increased. One of her favorites was *The Portrait of Doña Rosita Morillo* (1944). It was commissioned by Eduardo Morillo Safa, a patron of the arts who did much to advance Frida's career. More and more, she took commissions to help pay the bills and help support Rivera's dream of building Anahuacalli. Around this time, Frida also began to keep a diary in which she wrote down her most intimate thoughts. She continued to write a diary until her death.

In 1943, Frida and Rivera were both appointed to teach at the National School of Painting and Sculp-ture, which had opened only the year before in Mexi-co City. The school was known as La Esmeralda (meaning "The Emerald" in Spanish) by its students because it was originally located on a street with that name. Frida was excited about this opportunity and began teaching her students on campus. Her style of teaching was quite different compared to the other professors at La Esmeralda, as she had no formal art training. Instead of giving lectures to her students, she encouraged them to draw whatever they saw around them. She also treated her pupils as if they were her friends. Before long, Frida was forced to move her classes to the *Casa Azul* due to problems with her health. Eventually, most of her students found the

Frida and Diego Rivera are shown at right reading and working together in Frida's studio. One of Frida's most famous self-portraits, *The Two Fridas* (1939), hangs on the wall in the background.

journey to Coyoacán to be too far out of the way and dropped her class. Soon the only students she had left were Arturo García Bustos (1926-2017), Arturo Estrada Hernández (1925-   ), Guillermo Monroy (1924-   ), and Fanny Rabel (1922-2008). This small group became known as Los Fridos. These four artists continued to study under Frida's guidance at the *Casa Azul* and, years later, gained fame from their association with her.

Together with Rivera and some of his pupils, Frida would take her students on excursions, visiting different neighborhoods of Mexico City as well as the countryside. She taught them to find inspiration from scenes of everyday life and to appreciate the natural beauty of Mexico. Los Fridos often worked on projects together. One of their most famous was the mural they painted on the façade of a pulquería called La Rosita. (A pulquería is a type of tavern that serves a fermented drink made from a type of agave plant.) The mural was a great artistic and social success. Another of their murals was *Those Who Exploit Us and How They Exploit Us* (1945). This one was not well received. It reflected Communist themes that the artists felt were important to communicate to the public.

Role Reversal

Starting in 1944, Frida spent a good deal of her time in bed because of her poor health. She was almost always forced to wear a steel brace to support her weak spine. She wore a total of 28 different braces in the last 10 years of her life. Because of the terrible pain she was in, she stopped traveling to promote her art.

During this period, Frida painted many self-portraits in which she represented herself as ill or experiencing suffering in some way. One of the most famous of these self-portraits was *Broken Column* (1944). In it, Frida's spine is shown as an ancient, crumbling column, while the pain shooting throughout her body is represented by a series of sharp nails. Another example is *Without Hope* (1945). In this painting, Frida is in bed and isolated on a barren, rocky plain. This painting seems to express her frustration with the diet she was forced to endure to gain weight, which she found disgusting.

> *Frida painted many self-portraits in which she represented herself as ill or experiencing suffering in some way.*

In 1946, Frida underwent an operation on her spine in New York City. After that brief visit, she remained in Mexico for the rest of her life. Consequently, the *Casa Azul* became the center of her universe. She also lost her appetite and became very thin. At the time, there was much speculation about her physical condition. Some people whispered that all the operations she endured was Rivera's way of binding Frida to him. Even Dr. Eloesser thought many of them were unnecessary.

In September 1946, Frida received the National Prize of Arts and Sciences from the Ministry of Education for her painting titled *Moses* (1945). This work, more than any other, solidified her reputation in Mexico. In the painting, the infant Moses, who looks a little like her husband, bears the all-seeing third eye of wisdom (as Rivera does in many of her later works).

Floating down the Nile River, Moses is surrounded by images of the world's religions, Communism, and biological creation. Frida claimed she was inspired to do this painting after reading Sigmund Freud's book *Moses and Monotheism* (1939).

Around this time, Frida and Rivera's relationship underwent a great change. Frida, having gained fame as an artist in her own right, looked to Rivera as a professional role model less and less. She also started to act more as a protective and loving mother, rather than an obedient and passive wife. Photographs from this period reflect Frida's newfound self-confidence. She recorded her feelings about Rivera in her diary. "He's my child every minute, my newborn, every minute of the day, my very own," she wrote. This thinking seemed to allow Frida finally to come to terms with her husband's love affairs. Her new attitude also had a dramatic effect on Frida's work, and she expressed herself in surprising new ways. In *The Love Embrace of the Universe, the Earth (Mexico), Myself, Diego, and Señor Xólotl* (1949), Frida shows herself cradling Rivera in her arms the way a mother holds her child. Frida, in turn, is being embraced by Mother Earth, while the hand of the universe protects them all, including Señor Xólotl, Rivera's favorite dog.

Frida was not alone in recognizing the change in her marriage. Rivera himself understood that their roles were no longer the same as before. In 1947, he began a work titled *Dream of a Sunday Afternoon in Alameda Central Park*. It was his last great historical fresco and his most autobiographical. In the piece, Rivera represents himself as a young boy holding an

umbrella in one hand. The other hand is held by "Calavera Catrina," an elegantly dressed skeletal figure that represents the middle class. Frida stands behind Rivera, placing a hand on his shoulder in a motherly gesture. It was one of the finest portraits Rivera ever made of his beloved wife.

Failing Health

In 1950, Frida was in such poor health that she had to spend an entire year in the hospital, undergoing seven operations on her spine. It was not until November that she felt strong enough to paint again. That year, while still confined to her bed, she produced *The Kahlo Family Portrait*. As she worked on it, Rivera got a room for himself in the hospital next to Frida's and would often spend the night there. He tried to be as supportive as he could during this difficult time. However, he also kept busy with his own projects, continuing to do frescoes in the National Palace. When Frida was finally released from the hospital, she returned to the *Casa Azul*. But she was still very weak and in need of round-the-clock care. She dedicated a painting to her surgeon, Dr. Juan Farill, titled *Self-Portrait with a Portrait of Doctor Farill* (1951) in appreciation for his treatment. Almost like a devotional image (but with the doctor replacing the saint), Frida is shown holding a heart instead of an artist's palette.

As Frida's health continued to decline in the early 1950's, politics became a more important part of her life than ever before. She rejoined the Mexican Communist Party, but she rejected the influences of her onetime lover, Leon Trotsky, in favor of Joseph Stalin.

Diego Rivera's 1947 mural *Dream of a Sunday Afternoon in Alameda Central Park* (left) reflected a change in his and Frida's marriage. It shows him as a young boy and Frida standing behind him like a protective mother.

(The full extent of Stalin's cruel acts was not revealed by the Soviet government until after Kahlo's death.) Concerned that her work failed to reflect her political beliefs, Frida turned all her efforts toward serving the cause of the Revolution though her art. "I want to turn it into something useful," she wrote in her diary, "for up to now all I've done with it is to express myself." Her work went through another dramatic transformation. Instead of portraits, she began to produce still-life paintings with obvious references to Communism. Like Rivera, she depicted Stalin in her work as well as the dove of peace. At the same time, Frida admitted to Raquel Tibol, her official biographer, that her work was not as "revolutionary" as her husband's.

In April 1953, Frida had her first one-woman show in her home country. A dream of a lifetime had been fulfilled. The exhibition was held at the Gallery of Contemporary Art in Mexico City. It was made possible by her friend Lola Álvarez Bravo. Frida made a dramatic entrance. She was escorted by police cars with their sirens blaring, and she was carried into the gallery upon her four-post bed. She was excited about the show though she was very ill. Two months later, Frida returned to the hospital. In August of that year, her doctors told her there was nothing more they could do to heal her right leg. The gangrene was spreading, and her leg would have to be amputated below the knee. (Gangrene is the death of body tissue from lack of oxygen. It is caused by a loss of blood supply to areas of the body, often the hands or feet.) This news came as a shock to Frida. Despite all the pain her leg had caused her, she had fought her whole

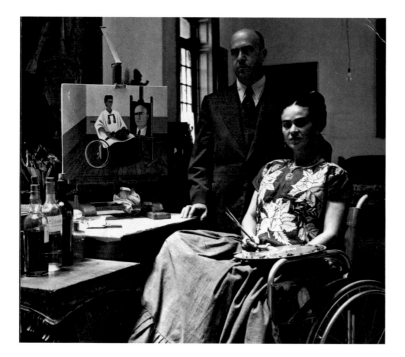

Frida dedicated *Self-Portrait with a Portrait of Doctor Farill* (1951) to her surgeon, Dr. Juan Farill (left, with Frida), in appreciation for his treatment. The painting sits on an easel in the background of this photograph.

life to keep it. Reluctantly, she agreed to have the operation.

Frida went into a deep depression after her surgery. Despite losing her leg and the terrible pain she endured, she learned to walk again with an artificial leg. She was forced to make repeated visits to the ABC Hospital during the last year of her life. Her love for Rivera, however, kept her going. Writing in her diary, Frida said, "I'll have enough strength to live for Diego, everything for Diego!" After months of not painting, she picked up her brush and began painting again. One of her last works of art was *Marxism Will Heal the Sick* (c. 1954). Her political convictions remained important until the end. On July 2, 1954, against her doctors' advice, she and Rivera attended a political demonstration to protest American military intervention in Guatemala. U.S. forces had overthrown the leftwing government of President Jacobo Árbenz. Unfortunately, attending the rally worsened Frida's condition. It would be her last public appearance. A photo taken of her that day shows her looking very frail. In fact, she was near death. As a final entry in her diary she wrote, "I hope that death will be easy, and I hope I won't come back." Her last drawing was of an angel wearing black boots ascending into the sky on green wings. On the evening of July 12, she developed a high fever and was in tremendous pain. The following morning, Frida Kahlo was found dead by her nurse. At the age of 47, she had died of a pulmonary embolism. (A pulmonary embolism is the sudden blockage of a major blood vessel in the lung, usually caused by a blood clot.)

On the evening of July 13, Frida's body lay in state in Mexico City's Palacio de Bellas Artes. She was wearing her favorite Tehuana-style dress, there were ribbons in her hair, and she was adorned with jewelry. Arturo García Bustos, one of Los Fridos, draped her

After Frida's death, her birthplace home, *Casa Azul* (below), was turned into the Frida Kahlo Museum. It contains artwork by Frida and Rivera and many of their artifacts, photographs, and personal items.

coffin in a Communist banner instead of the Mexican flag, causing a scandal. The following day, the coffin was carried through the rain amid a large crowd of mourners to the municipal cemetery's crematorium. Overcome with grief, Rivera wept openly. As Frida's body was placed in the crematorium, a strange thing happened. Her hair caught fire and began to glow like a wreath around her head, just as she had painted in a self-portrait that she had recently destroyed. After Frida's body was engulfed by the flames, Rivera made a sketch of her ashes. They were then placed in a pre-Columbian urn and taken to *Casa Azul*.

"Fridamania"

Frida Kahlo was an artist of undeniable talent, and her fame has only increased since her death. However, her work was nearly forgotten after she died, and it was several decades before she was "rediscovered" by the public. There are many possible reasons for this. Perhaps the images she used in her art were too shocking for the public to appreciate during her lifetime. For most of her life, she remained in the shadow of her famous husband, Diego Rivera. Many argue that Frida Kahlo was not taken seriously as an artist simply because she was a woman. Today, however, Kahlo attracts so much attention internationally that the term "Fridamania" has been used to describe her popularity.

Though Kahlo did not think of herself as a Surrealist, she is considered one of the first artists in that movement. During her lifetime, she produced some 200 self-portraits, many of which earn her the Surre-

Frida Kahlo's paintings were featured in a major exhibition at the Tate Modern in London in 2005. Exhibition curator Emma Dexter (center) stands in front of one of Frida's greatest masterpieces, *The Two Fridas* (1939). Dexter is wearing a cape with a large image of Frida on the back.

alist label, but her art was more than mere self-examination. It explored the pre-Columbian and Roman Catholic cultures of Mexico and shed light on suffering, illness, and death. Toward the end of her life, her work also expressed her Communist beliefs. Yet Kahlo's fame today has as much to do with her art as it does with the woman behind it. With her strong and charming personality, she had influence over some of the most powerful men of the political and art worlds of her day, including André Breton, Leon Trotsky, and Diego Rivera himself. The pain, drama, and tragedy of Frida Kahlo's life has made her more than just an artist. For many people across the world, she remains a social and political icon.

INDEX

FURTHER READING

Barbezat, Suzanne. *Frida Kahlo at Home.* Frances Lincoln, 2016.

Hillstrom, Laurie. *Frida Kahlo, Painter.* Lucent Pr., 2008.

Reef, Catherine. *Frida and Diego: Art, Love, Life.* Clarion, 2014.

Zavala, Adriana, and others, eds. *Frida Kahlo's Garden.* Prestel Pub., 2015.

ACKNOWLEDGMENTS

Cover: © Bettmann/Getty Images

3 Archives of American Art/ Smithsonian Institution

7-18 © Archivo Diego Rivera y Frida Kahlo, Banco de México, Fiduciario en el Fi deicomiso relativo a los Museos Diego Rivera y Frida Kahlo

21 Frida Kahlo

23 © Archivo Diego Rivera y Frida Kahlo, Banco de México, Fiduciario en el Fi deicomiso relativo a los Museos Diego Rivera y Frida Kahlo

25 Museo Frida Kahlo

26 © Alexandre Meneghini, AP/REX/ Shutterstock; © Alberto Pizzoli, AFP/ Getty Images

29 © Alberto Pizzoli, AFP/Getty Images

31 © Victor De Palma, The LIFE Images Collection/Getty Images

33 © SSPL/Getty Images

34 © John MacDougall, AFP/Getty Images

36 © Archivo Diego Rivera y Frida Kahlo, Banco de México, Fiduciario en el Fideicomiso relativo a los Museos Diego Rivera y Frida Kahlo

41 © Bettmann/Getty Images

45 © Paul Sancya, AP/REX/Shutterstock

48 © Bettmann/Getty Images

51 © Archivo Diego Rivera y Frida Kahlo, Banco de México, Fiduciario en el Fi deicomiso relativo a los Museos Diego Rivera y Frida Kahlo

54 © Omar Torres, AFP/Getty Images

57 © Bettmann/Getty Images

59 © Keystone-France/Getty Images

61 © AP/REX/Shutterstock; © Douglas Williams, age fotostock/SuperStock

64 © Dieter Nagl, AFPGetty Images

67 © Keystone/Getty Images

71-75 © Bettmann/Getty Images

77 © Dan Brinzac, New York Post Archives/Getty Images

79 © Graphic House/Getty Images

80 © Dan Brinzac, New York Post Archives/Getty Images

83 © Hulton Archive/Getty Images

86 © DEA/M. SEEMULLER/ Getty Images

89 Gisele Freund/Vicente Wolf Photography Collection/Salvador Dali Museum

90 © BondRocketImages/Shutterstock

92 © John D. McHugh, AFP/Getty Images